MAY 0 1 1998

NAPA CITY-COUNTY LIBRARY

3 1128 00727 0632

P9-CDB-158

PIONEER
CRAFTS

written by Barbara Greenwood

illustrated by Heather Collins

KIDS CAN PRESS LTD.

TORONTO

NAPA CITY-COUNTY LIBRARY
580 COOMBS STREET
NAPA, CA 94559-3396

Text copyright © 1997 by Barbara Greenwood
Illustrations copyright © 1997 by Heather Collins/Glyphics
Cover photograph copyright © 1997 by Sakulensky/Frost

All rights reserved. No part of this publication may be reproduced,
stored in a retrieval system or transmitted, in any form or by any means,
without the prior written permission of Kids Can Press Ltd. or,
in case of photocopying or other reprographic copying, a licence from
CANCOPY (Canadian Copyright Licensing Agency), 6 Adelaide Street East,
Suite 900, Toronto, ON, M5C 1H6.

Many of the designations used by manufacturers and sellers to distinguish their
products are claimed as trademarks. Where those designations appear in this
book and Kids Can Press Ltd. was aware of a trademark claim, the designations
have been printed in initial capital letters (e.g., Plasticine).

Neither the Publisher nor the Author shall be liable for any damage which may
be caused or sustained as a result of conducting any of the activities in this book
without specifically following instructions, conducting the activities without
proper supervision, or ignoring the cautions contained in the book.

Published in Canada by
Kids Can Press Ltd.
29 Birch Avenue
Toronto, ON M4V 1E2

Published in the U.S. by
Kids Can Press Ltd.
85 River Rock Drive, Suite 202
Buffalo, NY 14207

Edited by Laurie Wark
Designed by Marie Bartholomew and Karen Powers
Printed in Hong Kong by Wing King Tong Co. Ltd.

CM 97 0 9 8 7 6 5 4 3 2

Canadian Cataloguing in Publication Data

Greenwood, Barbara, 1940—
Pioneer crafts

(Kids can crafts)
ISBN 1-55074-359-7

1. Handicraft — Juvenile literature.
2. Pioneer children — Juvenile literature.
3. Frontier and pioneer life — Juvenile literature.
I. Collins, Heather.   II. Title.   III. Series.

TT160.G745   1997   j745.5   C96-932025-6

Contents

Introduction

Pioneer children were good at making things they needed for everyday life. Stores were far away and families had little money. So the children wove reeds and grasses into baskets, pieced together scraps of fabric for quilts, and made candles and lanterns to light their way in the dark forest.

Today we don't have to make our own cloth or tools as the early settlers did, but sometimes it's fun to make candles for a special occasion, weave gift baskets, or turn a piece of felt into cosy moccasins. In this book you'll find these and many more crafts you can do the pioneer way.

CARVING HINTS

Pioneer children used knives every day for such chores as shaving wood splints to start fires and cutting switches from trees to help herd the cows. Here are some tips on using knives safely for the carving projects in this book.

1 Sharp knives are safer to work with than dull knives. Ask an adult to sharpen your knife.

2 Hold the knife as though you were paring an apple. This lets you brace your thumb against the wood and gives you control over the amount you cut away.

3 For carving details, hold the knife as shown. You can control the knife better by holding the blade.

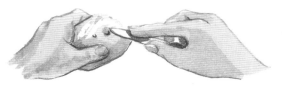

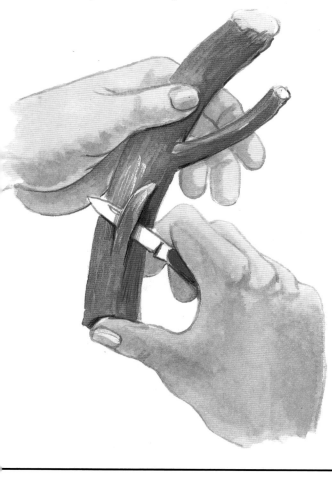

4 Hold the knife like this for making down cuts.

5 To sharpen an end, point the stick away from you. Holding the knife as shown, shave down the end. Cut away from your body.

SEWING HINTS

Pioneers sewed their own clothes and toys. To help you sew some of the crafts in this book, refer to these handy hints whenever you need to.

Threading a needle

1 Cut a piece of thread about the length of your arm.

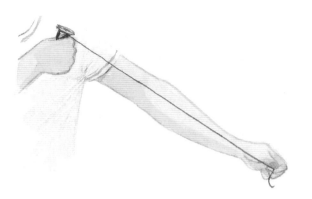

2 Wet one end of the thread in your mouth and poke it through the eye of the needle. Pull the thread until it is double.

3 Knot the end of the threads by wrapping them around your index finger, then rolling them off with your thumb.

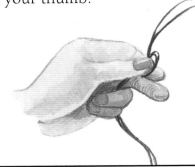

Running stitches

1 Push the needle up through the fabric, and pull it until the knot is against the underside of the fabric. If you are using heavy fabric or several layers, you might need a thimble on your middle finger to help you push the needle through.

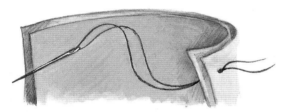

2 Poke the needle down, then bring it up about 1 cm (½ in.) along. Draw the thread through. Continue to sew tiny stitches in a straight row.

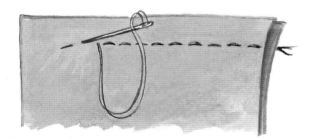

3 To finish, sew two or three stitches on top of the last one. Cut the thread.

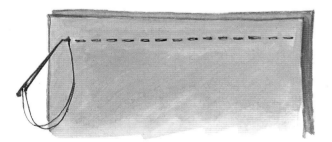

Overcast stitches

1 Push the needle up through the fabric and pull until the knot is against the underside of the fabric.

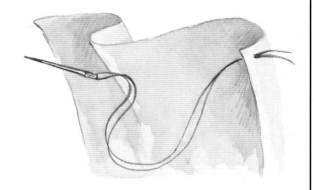

2 Bring the needle over the edge of the fabric and push it up through from the underside again. Keep the stitches close together and even.

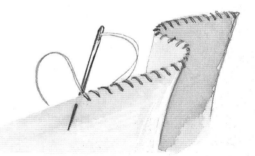

3 To finish, sew two or three stitches on top of the last one. Cut the thread.

Balancing acrobat

Early settlers had little time for fun in their busy days. But in the evenings, as they sat before the fire, out would come a jackknife to carve a wooden animal or make a clever toy like this balancing acrobat.

YOU WILL NEED

a round toothpick

a jackknife or paring knife

a bottle cork

markers

2 skewers or knitting needles

Plasticine or other modelling clay

a piece of string 1 m (3 ft.) long

1 Break a toothpick in half. Push the pointed end into the centre of one end of the cork. Let it stick out about 2.5 cm (1 in.). Make a notch in the end with a knife. This is the pivot.

2 Use markers to draw a face and clothes on the cork acrobat.

3 Stick the skewers into the sides of the cork at an angle, as shown. The angles must be the same.

5 Balance the acrobat on the tip of one finger by its pivot. If it falls off, it is not evenly weighted. Try adjusting the angle of the skewers or evening up the size of the balls.

4 Shape the Plasticine into two balls, each about 2.5 cm (1 in.) in diameter. They must be the same size. Stick them onto the ends of the skewers.

6 Ask two friends to hold the string tight. Balance the acrobat on the string. Raise or lower one end of the string to make the acrobat "walk."

Soap carving

Heaped beside the woodpile were wood ends that could be carved into toys for younger brothers and sisters. Soap is a good substitute for wood when you're learning how to carve.

a sharp paring knife or jackknife

a new bar of soap
(Ivory works well)

a sharp pencil and paper

carbon paper
(You can make carbon paper by scribbling on paper with a soft pencil.)

paper towel

1 Check page 5 for carving hints. Scrape down the front of the soap until it is smooth and flat.

2 On paper the same size as the side of the soap, draw the side view of an animal. On paper the same size as the thickness of the bar, draw the front view of an animal.

3 Lay the carbon paper (dark side down) over the bar and place the picture of the side view on top. With a sharp pencil, firmly trace the figure onto the soap. Repeat for the front view.

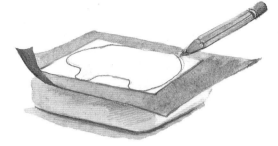

4 Taking small chunks at a time, cut the soap away from the figure. Leave about 0.5 cm (¼ in.) around the pencil line. Now you have a rough outline of the animal.

5 Look at your drawing and decide what areas have to be cut away (between the legs, for example). Look at the front view to see how to shape the muzzle and ears.

6 Use the point of the blade to add details to the eyes and hair.

7 Rub gently with paper towel to smooth and polish the surface.

Whimmy diddle

Run the wand up and down the stick of this favourite old toy, and watch the propeller spin first right, then left. It looks like magic, but it's really the changing vibrations along the stick that make the propeller change direction.

YOU WILL NEED

a jackknife

a branch about 20 cm (8 in.) long

a branch about 10 cm (4 in.) long

a twig 4 cm (1½ in.) long

a hammer

a small nail about 2.5 cm (1 in.) long

a sewing pin

1 See page 5 for carving hints, then sharpen one end of the long branch.

2 Starting about 4 cm (1½ in.) from the pointed end, cut seven evenly spaced notches.

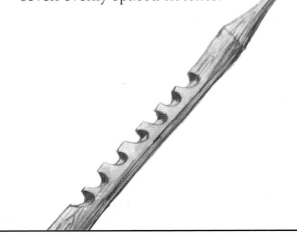

3 Carve the twig into a propeller.

4 Measure the propeller and mark the halfway point. Hammer the nail through the propeller at that mark. Remove the nail.

5 Push the pin through the hole in the propeller and into the sharpened end of the long branch. Leave some of the pin free so that the propeller can spin.

6 Sharpen one end of the short branch. This is the rubbing stick or wand.

7 Run the wand briskly along the notches towards the propeller. If the propeller does not spin, try carving the notches slightly deeper.

8 Practise running the wand up and down the notches until you can make the propeller spin and then change direction.

Spatter painting

Try decorating the pioneer way. Pioneers used spatter painting to brighten up wooden chairs and chests. You can use leaves or dry plants to spatter paint designs on gift boxes, bags, wrapping paper or cards.

YOU WILL NEED

leaves, ferns and grasses

newspaper

sheets of paper, bags, boxes or cards to decorate

a wire sieve or small square of wire screening

an old toothbrush or stiff-bristled paintbrush

tempera paint in several colours

1 For patterns, collect interesting shapes from nature. Use leaves while they are fresh, or press them between books to keep them flat.

2 Spread newspaper and place the paper or card for decorating on top. Arrange leaves in a pattern on the paper. Weigh each leaf down with erasers, balls of Plasticine or small stones.

3 Hold the sieve or screening about 8 cm (3 in.) above the paper. Dip the toothbrush into the paint, tap off any drips, then run the brush over the sieve. If you don't have a sieve or screening, hold the toothbrush over the paper and drag your finger along the bristles.

OTHER IDEAS

• For a feathery pattern, try outlining the image using an almost-dry brush. Dip the brush into the paint, then wipe most of the paint off on the newspaper. Holding a leaf down with your finger, brush from the pattern out to the paper.

4 Let the paint dry, then try spattering a second colour. When you are finished, carefully pick off the patterns.

Silhouette portrait

Before cameras were invented, the only way to have family portraits was to draw them or to make silhouettes. The silhouettes were coloured in with paint made from lampblack (the soot from candles). With the help of a friend, you can make a silhouette portrait.

YOU WILL NEED

white paper 25 cm x 30 cm
(10 in. x 12 in.)
(newsprint or any other large white paper can be used)

masking tape

a flashlight or adjustable desk lamp

a sharp pencil

black tempera paint

scissors

black construction paper or bristol board

white paper or bristol board

glue

1 Ask permission to attach the large white paper to a wall with masking tape. Draw the curtains so the room is dark.

2 Have your friend sit on a chair sideways to the paper. You're going to trace the side view, or profile, of his or her face.

3 Place the light so that it shines on your friend's profile and casts a shadow on the paper. Move your friend farther from or closer to the wall until the shadow on the paper is the size you want.

4 With the pencil, carefully trace the outline on the paper.

5 This profile can either be painted black or cut out. To cut it out, place black construction paper behind the traced profile. Holding the two sheets of paper together, cut around the profile.

6 Glue the black silhouette onto a sheet of white paper or bristol board.

OTHER IDEAS

• If you want a smaller profile, reduce the outline profile on a photocopier. Then paint it or cut it out as in step 5.

Punched-tin lantern

Pioneers often had to milk the cows or harness the horses early in the morning or late at night. To light up the dark barn but keep the hay safe from fire, they carried candles inside tin lanterns.

18

YOU WILL NEED

a clean can with one end removed at least 398 mL (14 oz.) in size

a felt-tip marker

a towel

nails of different sizes

a hammer

a piece of wire about 30 cm (12 in.) long

a short candle or tealight

matches

1 Fill the can with water and place it in the freezer. Leave it until the water is frozen solid. The ice will give a hard surface against which to hammer your pattern.

2 Use the marker to draw a simple design on the can.

3 Lay the can on its side on a folded towel. Using the various sizes of nails, hammer the design into the tin.

4 For the handle, hammer a hole on either side of the can near the top.

5 Loosen the ice with hot water and remove it. Dry the can. Thread the wire through the handle holes and bend the ends up.

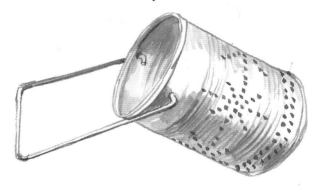

6 Have an adult light the candle and drip a few drops of wax into the can. Put out the candle. Let the wax cool slightly, then stand the candle in the wax. Let the wax harden.

Be careful of the punched tin inside the can — it can be sharp.

7 Carefully light the candle and see how the punched designs throw patterns onto the walls in a dark room.

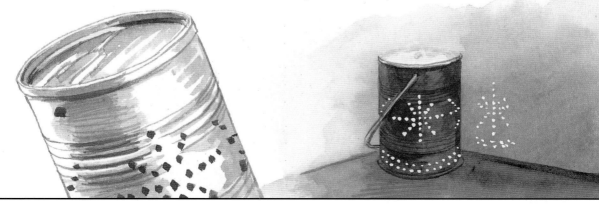

Weaving a basket

On pioneer farms children gathered nuts in small baskets, and Mother used large baskets to store apples and potatoes. Many baskets were bought from Native people, who were experts at weaving them from reeds, bark and vines. Try weaving with cardboard, then look for reeds or bulrushes to make more baskets.

thin, sturdy cardboard in 1 or 2 colours (*file folders, cereal boxes or bristol board*)

scissors

a pencil

corrugated cardboard or Styrofoam about 20 cm (8 in.) square

push pins

cardboard 10 cm (4 in.) square (*cereal box*)

brown paper bags or wrapping paper

glue or tape

1 From the thin cardboard, cut 26 pieces called splints, each 40 cm x 0.5 cm (16 in. x ¼ in.). Put a pencil mark halfway along two of the splints.

2 Using the corrugated cardboard as a pad to push the pins into, lay the marked splint 1 across splint 2, and fasten them with a pin.

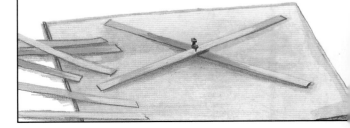

3 Add a splint on either side of splint 1 under splint 2. Weave splints on either side of splint 2, going over and under the other splints. Pin a few splints down to keep them from shifting.

4 Continue weaving until the bottom of your basket is the same size as the 10-cm (4-in.) square of cardboard. Remove the push pins, place the cardboard square over the basket bottom and pin it at each corner.

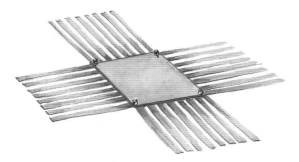

5 Fold each splint at the edge of the square so that it stands up.

6 For the sides of the basket, cut 5 or 6 weaver strips from the paper bags, each 50 cm x 1 cm (20 in. x ½ in.).

7 Place a weaver strip behind one upright splint and glue or tape it in place. Weave over and under the splints around the basket. Crease the weaver at each corner. Glue or tape the end behind the first splint. Cut off any extra length.

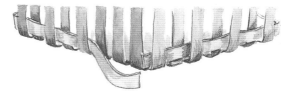

8 For the second row, start several splints over. Continue to add weavers until the basket is as tall as you want. Unpin the basket and remove the cardboard square.

9 To finish off the top of the basket, find the splints that pass over the last weaver. Fold each one over the weaver to the inside of the basket and weave it under the third row.

10 Every second splint should still be standing up. Fold each towards the outside of the basket, and weave it under the third row. Cut each off just below the weaver.

Moulded candles

Pioneer families made everyday candles by dipping wicks into melted animal fat called tallow. For special occasions they made moulded candles from the waxy coating of bayberries or from beeswax. You can make moulded candles for your own special occasion.

YOU WILL NEED

a large pot

2 sticks of paraffin wax
(from a grocery or craft store)

an empty 1.36-L (48-oz.) can
with one end removed

broken bits of crayon *(optional)*

3 waxed paper cups or
2 1-L (1-qt.) milk cartons

scissors

candlewick or heavy cotton string

masking tape

pencils

newspaper

oven mitts

1 Pour water into the pot to a depth of 5 cm (2 in.). Ask an adult to place the pot on the stove and turn on the burner. When the water is hot, turn the burner to a low heat.

2 Place the paraffin wax in the can and place the can in the pot. For coloured candles, peel the paper from three or four bits of crayon and add them to the can. The wax and crayon will take about five minutes to melt.

3 For moulds, use waxed paper cups, or milk cartons cut down to 8 cm (3 in.).

4 For each candle cut a piece of candlewick 8 cm (3 in.) longer than the mould is tall. Use masking tape to stick the wick to the bottom of the mould.

5 Roll the top end of the wick around the pencil. Rest the pencil on the rim of the mould.

6 Place the mould on several layers of newspaper on a flat surface. Ask an adult to pour melted wax into the mould. Leave the moulded candle to harden.

7 When the wax is hard, peel the paper cup or milk carton away from the candle. Cut the wick so that only 1 cm (½ in.) sticks up.

Crazy quilt

Log cabins were cold and drafty, so beds needed many blankets. Since fabric was hard to come by, pioneers saved even tiny pieces. They sewed the scraps together to make blankets. Because the patches came in a jumble of colours, the quilts were called crazy quilts. You can quilt a doll's blanket or a cushion cover.

YOU WILL NEED

a pencil, ruler and paper

sewing pins

fabric scraps in several colours

scissors

a needle and thread

stuffing
(extra layers of fabric, cotton batting or polyester batting)

a darning needle

yarn

1 Decide how to arrange your colours by drawing a large square and dividing it into nine squares. The easiest design is a checkerboard.

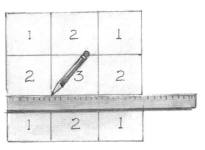

2 To make a sewing pattern, draw a 10-cm (4-in.) square on a piece of paper. This will give you a finished quilt about 30 cm x 30 cm (12 in. x 12 in.).

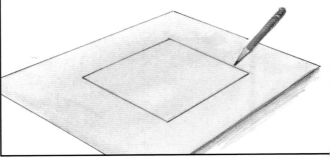

3 Pin the pattern to your fabric and cut out the square. Cut eight more in the colours needed for your design.

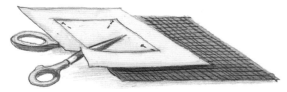

4 Sew the first three squares together as shown, making each seam 0.5 cm (¼ in.) wide. Repeat for the second and third rows.

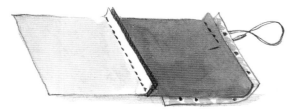

5 Sew the three rows together. Ask an adult to iron the seams flat, if necessary. This is the front of your quilt.

6 To make the back, cut a square the same size as the front. Place the front and back together with right sides facing each other. Sew around three sides 0.5 cm (¼ in.) from the edges.

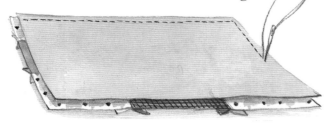

7 Cut a square of stuffing 1 cm (½ in.) smaller around than the quilt cover. Place the stuffing on the back square of your quilt and pin it in place. Turn the quilt right side out.

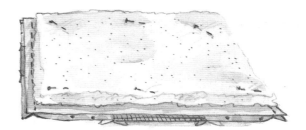

8 Take out the pins and use them to pin through the front, the stuffing and the back. Turn the bottom edges inside and sew with overcast stitches.

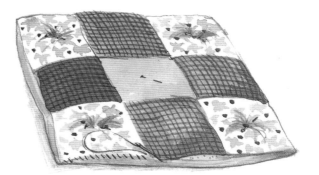

9 To hold the stuffing in place, thread a darning needle with yarn. At the corner of each square, stitch through the front and back covers. Draw the yarn through and cut it, leaving two 1-cm (½-in.) tails. Tie them in knots and remove the pins.

Rug braiding

Fabric was never thrown away in pioneer homes. Scraps were kept in a rag bag to make a quilt or a rag rug. For a rug, strips of fabric were tightly braided, then coiled and sewn into a circle or oval. You can braid a rug for a doll's house or a trivet to set under a teapot.

YOU WILL NEED

thick fabric from an old blanket, worn-out jeans or sweatpants

scissors

a needle and thread

a safety pin

a darning needle

1 Tear or cut the fabric into a number of strips 5 cm (2 in.) wide. Sew strips together with running stitches until you have three strips each about 1 m (3 ft.) long.

2 Fold the strips in half lengthwise, then fold each edge into the middle.

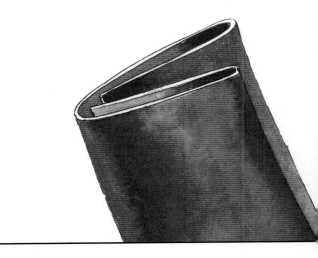

3 Place the folded strips one on top of another, and sew them together.

4 Have someone hold the sewn ends of your strips while you braid a section 25 cm (10 in.) long. Keep the strips folded and braid tightly to make a strong, firm strand.

5 Continue braiding until you are about 8 cm (3 in.) from the end. Pin the three strands together so they won't loosen. Then sew more strips to each end. Unpin the braid and continue.

6 When the braid is about 1 m (3 ft.) long, pin the end. Thread the darning needle and pull it through the beginning section of the braid. On a table, hold this end down and wind the braid into a tight coil.

7 Holding the coil in place, sew the edges together. Continue coiling and sewing until the circle is the size you want. While sewing, keep the coiled braid flat so that the edges won't curl up.

8 To finish, take out the pin, fold the three strands under and sew them together with a running stitch. Use overcast stitching to sew this end to the braided coil.

Moccasins

In pioneer days, boots made by shoemakers were expensive and difficult to repair. Some families used an idea from the Native people and sewed moccasins from deerskin. Padded with thick socks, these made walking through the forest warm and comfortable. You can make moccasins for yourself from modern materials.

YOU WILL NEED

newspaper

a marker and ruler

fabric, such as felt, fake leather, upholstery fabric or canvas

scissors

embroidery floss or beads *(optional)*

a needle
(for heavy material use a big needle)

strong thread

sewing pins

1 Place your bare foot on a piece of newspaper and trace around it.

2 Draw a pattern around the traced foot similar to the one shown. To find the distance from 1 to 2 and from 3 to 4, measure across your instep and divide that number in half.

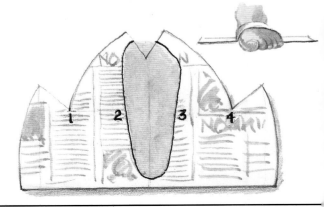

3 Pin the pattern on the fabric, trace around it and cut it out. Trace and cut a second one.

4 If you want to decorate the flaps, now is the time to do it. You can draw designs with markers, embroider designs, or sew on beads.

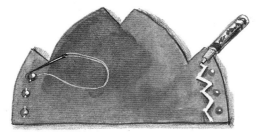

5 Fold one moccasin in half with right sides facing in. Use running stitches to sew the top. Gather the stitches slightly to fit the shape of your foot. End off with several overlapping stitches.

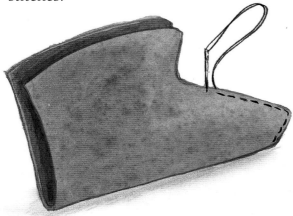

6 Turn the moccasin right side out and try it on. Use pins to fit the heel seam. Take the moccasin off and sew the seam with running stitches to 2 cm (¾ in.) from the bottom. Trim the seam.

7 Cut out a square as shown. Flatten the heel and sew it closed with overcast stitching.

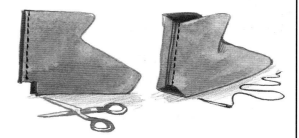

8 To make the ties, cut two strips of fabric, each 1 cm (½ in.) wide and 38 cm (15 in.) long.

9 Wrap the ties around your ankles under the flaps, and tie them at the back. Be careful walking on slippery floors.

Making a loom

Pioneer children learned to weave on small looms. They made ties for bonnets, braces to hold up pants, and fabric squares to stitch together for blankets or shawls. You can make a simple loom to weave hair bands, bookmarks or afghan squares.

YOU WILL NEED

stiff cardboard
(cereal boxes work well)

a pencil and ruler

scissors

a Styrofoam or cardboard tray

yarn

1 To make the bobbin, draw a rectangle on the cardboard 4 cm x 8 cm (1½ in. x 3 in.). Draw a line 1 cm (½ in.) from each end. Use these lines as guides to cut the curved ends of the bobbin.

bobbin

2 To make the heddle, draw a rectangle on the cardboard 2.5 cm (1 in.) wide and 4 cm (1½ in.) longer than the width of your tray. Cut it out, making a point at one end.

heddle

3 To make the loom, mark the centre of one end of your tray. To the left of the centre, mark half the width you want your finished piece to be and make a small cut. Do the same to the right.

4 Measure and mark the other end the same way, but don't cut it.

5 To dress the loom, knot the end of the yarn and slip it into the notch at the bottom left of the loom.

6 Starting from the top left-hand mark, wind the yarn around the loom. Lay the strands side by side. Continue winding until you reach the mark on the right side. Make sure you have an even number of strands.

7 Slip the last strand in the notch on the right-hand side. Cut the yarn, leaving a 2.5-cm (1-in.) tail.

8 Cut 2 m (6 ½ ft.) of yarn and wind it onto the bobbin. Tie a knot in the end of the bobbin yarn. Slip the knotted end into the left-hand notch on the loom. Now turn the page to find out how to weave.

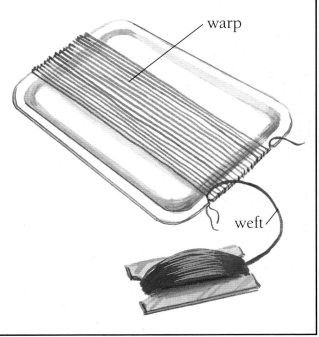

warp

weft

Weaving

Some pioneer families had a large loom set up in an attic room or out in the barn. Often one child would learn to work this loom to make woven rugs or cloth of wool and linen.

1 Using the pointed end of the heddle, weave it over the first strand and under the next strand. Continue weaving to the end.

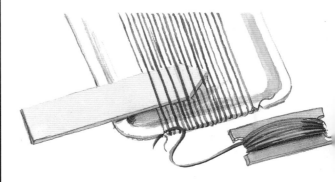

2 Turn the heddle on edge so that it makes a space between the two sets of strands. This space is called the shed.

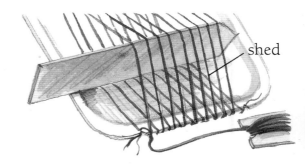

shed

3 Slide the bobbin of yarn through the shed, and pull the yarn not quite tight.

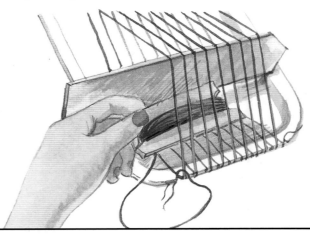

4 Turn the heddle so that it lies flat. Push it against the woven yarn until the yarn lies evenly along the top of the loom. This is called beating the weft.

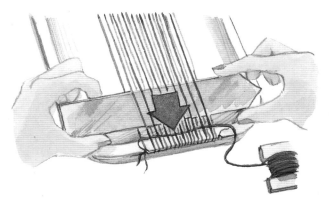

5 Take the heddle out. This time, weave it *under* the first strand and *over* the next strand. Continue to the end.

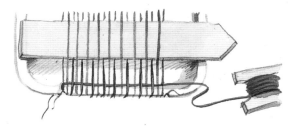

6 Repeat steps 2 through 5 working from left to right, then right to left, until the woven piece is the length you want.

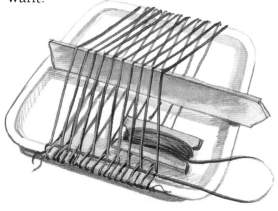

7 If you want the piece longer than the loom, slip the knots out of the notches. Slide the woven section over the top edge of the loom until the unwoven strands are on the upper side of the loom. Continue weaving.

8 To finish, turn the loom over and cut across the strands at the back. Tie strands 1 and 3 together, then strands 2 and 4. Continue tying across the width. Do this at both ends.

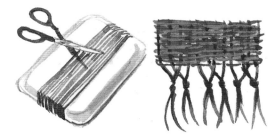

9 Cut the extra strands off just beyond the knots, or leave them as a fringe.

OTHER IDEAS

• Experiment with design. By using two colours alternately in the warp and the weft, you can make a checked pattern.

Dyeing

Pioneers gathered leaves, flowers and roots to dye yarn or fabric. Yellow from onion skins, green from lily of the valley leaves, or pink from madder roots were pretty, but the most practical colours for work clothes were brown or black from acorns or the bark of the logwood tree. You can dye a pair of cotton socks, then use them to make the doll on page 36.

them to make the doll on page 36.

YOU WILL NEED

a kettle

100 g (¼ lb.) of loose tea or 18 tea bags

2 pots

a sieve or colander

a pair of white cotton tube socks

1 Bring 1 L (4 c.) of water to a boil in the kettle.

2 Put the tea in one pot and cover with the boiling water. Let the tea steep for 15 minutes.

3 Hold the sieve over the second pot. Pour the tea into the second pot and let it cool. Throw out the tea leaves.

4 Wet the socks with clean water, then wring them out so they are damp but not dripping.

5 Place the socks in the tea dye. If necessary, add enough cool water to cover them. Simmer on low heat for 10 minutes. The longer you simmer the socks the deeper the colour will be.

6 Rinse the socks in hot water and then cool water. Keep rinsing until the water is clear. Hang the socks to dry inside or in a shady place outside. Sunlight will bleach the colour.

OTHER IDEAS

• You can use the same dyeing instructions with other plants to create different colours. Use 1 kg (2 lb.) of onion skins to make yellow dye or marigold flowers to make brown dye. Before you dye your fabric, you must add a colour fixer or mordant. (Tea provides its own mordant.) To make the mordant, mix 5 mL (1 tsp.) of alum and 2 mL (½ tsp.) of washing soda (not baking soda) in 4 L (1 gal.) of water. Before dyeing, soak the cloth in this mixture overnight. Use rubber gloves when you wring out the fabric to prevent the mordant from drying your skin.

onion skins

lily of the valley leaves

wild madder root

marigold flowers

Sewing a doll

In early days, dolls were usually homemade. A square of cloth wrapped around a wooden spoon or a corncob would make a baby doll. An older child might whittle a doll from a piece of wood. But the most cuddly dolls were sewn from rag-bag scraps. You can make a rag doll from the socks you dyed on page 34.

YOU WILL NEED

a pair of cotton tube socks
(dyed or undyed)

scissors

a pencil and ruler

stuffing
(discarded pantyhose or cotton batting)

a needle and thread

yarn

glue

fabric paint, felt or buttons

1 Cut off the cuff of one sock. Measure and divide your sock into thirds. The top third, starting at the toe, will be the head. Make a pencil line on both sides to mark the head.

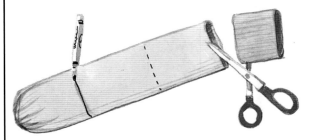

2 Stuff the head. Put your hand inside the sock to hold it open. Sew a running stitch along the pencil line.

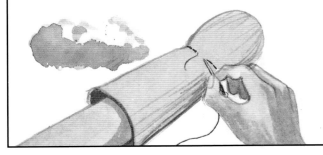

3 Pull the thread tight to create the neck. Wrap the thread two or three times around the neck. Finish with several overlapping stitches and cut the thread.

4 Stuff the body. Close the bottom edge with overcast stitches.

5 Cut off the cuff and toe of the second sock. Cut the remaining piece in quarters to make the arms and legs.

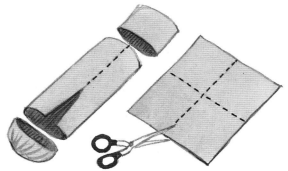

6 Turn one leg piece inside out. Sew down the side and along one end, curving the end as shown.

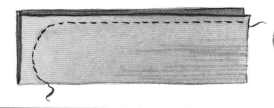

7 Turn the leg right side out and stuff it. Close the top end with overcast stitching.

8 Repeat for the second leg and the two arms. Use overcast stitching to sew them onto the body.

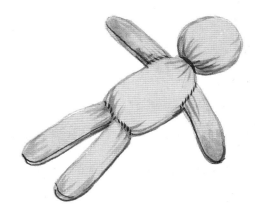

9 To make the hair, divide 21 strands of yarn, each 45 cm (18 in.) long, into three groups and braid them. Tie each end with yarn or ribbon. Sew the braid across the head.

10 To make the face, glue on felt eyes and a mouth, sew on buttons, or draw with fabric paint.

Doll clothes

In a pioneer home every piece of clothing was made by hand. Even a six-year-old would know how to sew. Making dolls and doll clothes was a good way to practise sewing skills. Here's how to dress the rag doll you made on page 36.

YOU WILL NEED

a pencil, paper and ruler

scissors

fabric pieces

sewing pins

a needle and thread

a large-eyed needle

yarn

1 Place your doll on the paper and outline its body, legs and arms. Cut out half of the drawing to use as a pattern.

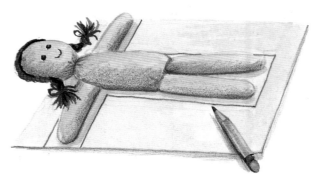

2 Fold the fabric in half. Make a pencil mark 2.5 cm (1 in.) from the fold (or more for a fuller dress). Pin the pattern on the fabric so that the straight edge lines up with the fold.

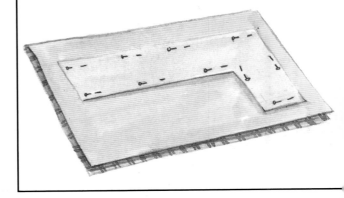

3 Leaving 0.5 cm (¼ in.) for a seam, cut around the outside edges of the pattern. Do not cut the folded side. Cut a second piece the same way.

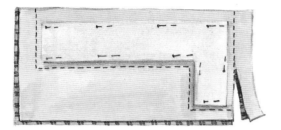

4 Unfold the two pieces. With right sides facing in, pin them together. Using running stitches, sew up the side and shoulder seams. Clip the underarm seams to keep them from puckering.

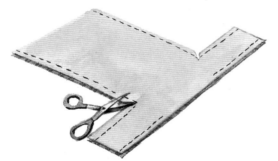

5 Turn the dress right-side out. Pin up the bottom edge and the sleeves 0.5 cm (¼ in.) for a hem, and sew with running stitches.

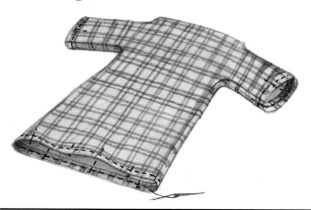

6 At the neckline, turn the edges under about 0.5 cm (¼ in.) and pin them flat.

7 Thread the large-eyed needle with yarn. Do not make a knot at the end. Beginning at the centre front, use running stitches to sew the neckline. Leave 5-cm (2-in.) tails at both ends.

8 Put the dress on the doll, and pull both ends of the yarn to gather it at the neck. Tie the ends in a bow. Turn the page to find out how to make an apron and bonnet for your doll.

Apron and bonnet

1 To make an apron for your doll, cut a rectangle twice the width of the doll. Hem the sides with running stitches.

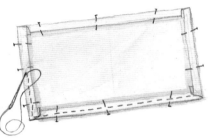

2 Cut a piece of yarn twice the width of the apron. Using running stitches, sew across the top of the apron, leaving tails. Gather and tie the apron on to the doll.

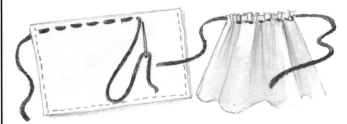

3 To make a bonnet, cut a rectangle 15 cm x 40 cm (6 in. x 16 in.). Fold and sew two right sides together as shown.

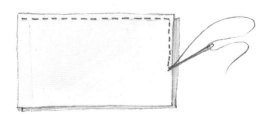

4 Turn right side out, fold in half again and use running stitches to sew the back seam. Turn it inside out.

5 Fold back the brim and try the bonnet on the doll. Mark where the ties should go.

6 Cut two yarn ties, each 8 cm (3 in.) long. Sew the ties to the bonnet.